GREAT NORTH of SCOTLAND RAILWAY

and

HIGHLAND RAILWAY

HISTORICAL MAPS

R. A. COOK

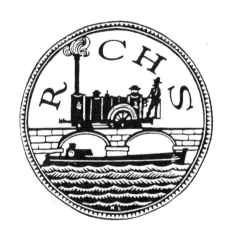

1977

Railway & Canal Historical Society

Published 1977 by the Railway & Canal Historical Society,
34 Manor Avenue, Caterham, Surrey CR3 6AN, and distributed
by the Hon. Sales Officer, J.W.D. Miller, 11 Burleigh Road,
West Bridgford, Nottingham NG2 6FP

SBN 901461 22 9

Introduction

The purpose of this booklet is to show the building-up of the Great North of Scotland Railway and the Highland Railway until their separate identities were lost in the 1923 grouping—the Great North of Scotland to become part of the L.N.E.R., and the Highland a part of the L.M.S.R.

With these two smaller companies it has been found more convenient to make a combined volume, although the two companies' lines are the subject of separate mapwork as follows:

GNS 1	West Central
GNS 2	Central
GNS 3	East Coast
GNS 4	Aberdeen-Ballater
HR 1	Northern lines
HR 2	West Central
HR 3	East Central
HR 4	Southern lines to the connection with the C.R. line from Perth to Aberdeen.

As far as is known the maps show every section of line owned or worked by the companies, but it is admitted that there may be omissions or slight errors of placement. An 'out-of-scale' approach has been adopted in order to clarify small areas where confusion could arise either for siting or dating. The dates shown are those on which each section of line first carried public revenue-earning traffic. Only the last two digits of the year are shown, but since the dates are limited in period to 1850-1921, no confusion can arise. Thus 3-7-62 is 3rd July 1862, and 1-7-03 is 1st July 1903.

All junction names have been taken from official documents and care has been taken to avoid the use of unofficial names, although space precludes the showing of all named junctions. It is for this reason also that no attempt has been made to show intermediate stations. Details of Acts have been extracted from the 'Index to Local and Personal Acts 1801-1947', and the Royal Assent dates from the most authoritative sources available.

The author makes no claim to original research on these companies, merely presentation. The history of both companies has been accurately covered in book form, and in articles, by the late H.A. Vallance, whilst the G.N. of S. has been the subject of a special issue by the Stephenson Locomotive Society. Further source material has been extracted from 'Locomotive and Train Working in the Latter Part of the 19th Century', Volume 3, by the late E.L. Ahrons.

Acknowledgement must, however, be made to Mr. M.D. Greville, who initially checked the historical content and Act section of the G.N. of S., and to Mr. C.R. Clinker, who has very kindly checked the complete and finalised proofs, and for valued comment. Details of the Brora Colliery Tramway have been extracted from an article by Mr. Iain D.O. Frew in the 'Railway Magazine' for January 1960.

R.A. COOK
November 1976

Historical sketch

The Great North of Scotland Railway and the Highland Railway are Britain's two most northerly railway companies, and in route mileage rank 16th and 13th respectively. In character they are very different, with the G.N. of S. being concentrated in Aberdeenshire, where it had a virtual monopoly, with but two isolated 'limbs', one to Boat of Garten, and one to a terminus at Ballater. The coastal area northwards from Aberdeen, around the tip of Aberdeenshire at Fraserburgh, and then westwards towards the Moray Firth and Inverness, was not the sparsely-populated area in 1840 that we know today. Fishing has always been a major industry centred around Aberdeen but many smaller ports or harbours provided the refuge for smaller fishing fleets of both inshore and sea-going vessels. There were also many small industries set up by the crofters, and outlets for any products from this area relied on the few tracks which passed for roads, and the natural sea outlet by the relatively shallow, but treacherous, waters of the North Sea. With the coming of the railway a third outlet became available, although the topography of the coastline prevented direct connections to many of these small industries and resort had to be made to cartage to the nearest railhead. The G.N. of S. were very jealous of their holding and managed to cling grimly to their monopoly by the promotion of nominally independent companies to keep out the rival Highland Railway.

The Highland Railway was also a monopolistic concern and the sprawl of its metals resembled, in general shape, that of the Celtic cross with its centre at Inverness. From this point it had a short eastward limb to Keith, where it joined the G.N. of S., and a long westward one to Kyle of Lochalsh. Its southern extremity took it to a junction with the main line of the Caledonian Railway from Perth to Aberdeen at Stanley, almost on the same latitude as Dundee, whilst its northern limb took it to the tip of Scotland at Thurso on the Pentland Firth, although its main line was to Wick, on the eastern coast. In the course of its wanderings it had the distinction of reaching the highest main line railway summit in the British Isles at Druimuachdar—1,484ft. above sea level. Not only did it reach this summit, but in so doing it conquered both the Cairngorms and the Grampians in its passage (the extreme northern areas of Scotland being not so rugged in a relative sense).

The Scots of the North were very much Highlanders, and it was to the Highland capital of Inverness that the railways were to aim. In this sense the Highland were successful, whereas the G.N. of S. were not, and it was to Inverness that the produce of the clan communities travelled. Even so the area was still a sparsely-populated one and journeys to the rail link were by no means easy. The northern towns of Thurso and Wick became the major centres for the transport southwards of the fish netted by the coastal fishermen, and of those further North in the Orkneys and the Shetlands by means of the sea links.

Initially, the companies promoted were essentially local ones to interlink the various communities, but as these themselves connected into through routes, it became apparent that a central body was required to run the entire system. It was from this that the Highland Railway was born, unlike the G.N. of S., which was a mainly autonomous company.

Whereas the G.N. of S. was built to follow the various valleys and the flatter landscape of the East coast, the Highland was the complete opposite. It is on the line northwards from Stanley to Inverness, and the western end of the line to Kyle of Lochalsh, that some of the grandest views of the rugged Scottish scenery can be found. Indeed, it has been said that the only way to see the Pass of Killiecrankie was by rail. The western limb to Kyle was a major feat of engineering to its terminus at Strome Ferry, the remaining ten miles into Kyle itself being a daunting prospect. It was from Strome Ferry that steamer services operated to Skye and the Western Isles. The line abounded in steep gradients and was very costly to build, even more so when the final section to Kyle was being built through several solid rock cuttings, and it was almost 30 years before the final section was opened to a pier at Kyle, to which the steamer services were re-routed.

The G.N. of S. had no such grandeur to call upon, but one of the places served was the Royal residence at Balmoral, the station for which was at Ballater, and at least they could boast the 'Queen's Messenger Express'. Both railways were products of the Railway Mania period and both suffered during the financial crisis which followed. In fact when calls were made on the subscribers to the G.N. of S. it was found that no money was forthcoming and the planned start was delayed by a considerable period of time. As part of its route the company had purchased the Aberdeenshire Canal in 1845 for the first part of the line towards Huntly. When the first section was opened in 1854 it was felt by the local population that the canal would have been better left alone as a more reliable and quicker mode of travel.

A further factor in these comparatively late promotions was not only the lack of finance, but the absence both of local resources to justify their existence, and the lack of technical know-how necessary to build the lines.

The G.N. of S. were thwarted in their bid to link Aberdeen and Inverness by two factors: firstly, lack of finance to start the construction of the railway, and finally, by the promotion of the independent Inverness and Nairn Railway, and it was not until 1862 that the company finally opened to Elgin and was allowed running powers into Inverness. In 1847 the company had obtained an Act to amalgamate with the Aberdeen Railway, but this was annulled in 1850 and the Aberdeen Railway, which was looking in a more southerly direction, became amalgamated with the Scottish Midland Railway to form the Scottish North Eastern Railway in 1856. In 1863 the Inverness and Perth Junction Railway opened its direct line south from Forres, giving a direct route to Perth avoiding the circuitous route via Aberdeen which, at that time, had no interconnection between the termini of the G.N. of S. and the Scottish North Eastern. Although this link was opened in 1864, the following year saw the amalgamation of the lines to Elgin, from Inverness, and the line to Stanley, as the Highland Railway.

Thus the G.N. of S. became totally isolated and the seeds were sown for the company to become the naughty little boy whose toys had been taken away. In Aberdeen this resulted in the timing of train departures to coincide with the distant appearance of passengers hurrying from the Guild Street terminus of the Scottish North Eastern to catch the north-bound connection. At this point the platforms were closed and the connection departed, much to the chagrin of the perspiring passengers. However, the staff on one occasion were either over-zealous, or else not forewarned, and succeeded in trapping one of their own Directors on the wrong side of the barrier, and the end of this part of the feuding was in sight.

To the West, however, it was not the end and the feud continued for several years more. It has been said that the two Boards occasionally met to iron out difficulties, but that ten minutes was about the limit of any cordiality; they were just not compatible. As the inimitable pen of the late E.L. Ahrons puts it—in what must be a very free adaptation of Bret Harte:

'Then McTavish of Cromarty, raised a point of order when

A chunk of Scottish granite hit him in the abdomen,

He smiled a sickly sort of smile, and curled up on the floor,

And the subsequent proceedings interested him no more.'

The logical conclusion from this is that whatever the differences were between them, the granite referred to was of the Aberdeen variety and the naughty G.N. of S. was being rude to its neighbours, and the Highlanders would not take kindly to this sort of treatment. When, eventually, a more moderate policy prevailed, the question of amalgamation was raised on several occasions and at the last of these, in 1905, the G.N. of S. Directors were in favour; but there was a general apathy amongst the Highland Board and the scheme came to naught.

Both lines were essentially single track with passing loops at certain stations, as befitted the terrain and the sparseness of the population. However, towards the latter end of the nineteenth century, extensive doubling was commenced and went on through the First World War period until 1921. During the war both companies were called upon to transport vast quantities of coal, stores and personnel for transhipment to the Grand Fleet's major wartime base at Scapa Flow in the Orkneys. This traffic severely taxed the rolling stock and locomotives of both companies, and many other companies' stock found its way to the North on through traffic. On the G.N. of S. forestry camps were set up at Kemnay, Knockando and Nethy Bridge, to provide timber for sleepers and pit props. Sidings were built to them but the camps were under the control of the Canadian Forestry Corps with assistance from German prisoners-of-war. A further line was opened in 1915, to the airship base at Lenabo, from Longside. This line was operated by Royal Flying Corps personnel. On the Highland the line to the North became saturated, and there were additional military facilities set up at Muirtown Basin and at Dalmore, 4 miles from Invergordon, where a mine base was constructed at a distillery, and new lines and a pier were started in 1918 in connection with the northern mine barrage. On the line from Kyle, heavy trains, usually headed by locomotives from other companies, toiled over the gradients carrying materials shipped from America for the minefield mentioned earlier.

Before describing the train services of the two companies it will be easier to dispose of the shipping activities. The G.N. of S. restricted this to services begun in 1859, one from Invergordon to Inverness, and another taking in the Moray Firth ports, Aberdeen and Granton. The patronage of these was so poor that the service ceased after a ten-month trial period. For its part the Highland ran two services, the first of these from Scrabster to the ports of Stromness and Kirkwall on Orkney. This service began around 1880 but was short-lived and passed to local and more established concerns. When the line was opened to Strome Ferry in 1870 a service was established to the islands of Skye and Lewis, which continued until 1880, when the service was taken over by the then well-established firm of David MacBrayne. All services had been disposed of by 1882.

Despite the comparatively short life of even the latter service, the Highland managed at least one distinction from it. When the steamer 'Ferret' was taken out of service in 1880 it was sent to the Clyde for sale, and it was from there that it was hired on charter and hijacked, eventually finding its way to Australia, only to be seized by Customs at Melbourne. It ended its days there, being wrecked off Cape Yorke in 1920. Unfortunately for the company there were still several Highland Railway employees on board, and quite naturally they wished to receive wages for the period whilst in 'custody'. A period of three years of litigation followed, with the outcome that their entitlement was paid.

When the G.N. of S. was opened, its train services were more akin to a funeral procession than a public service. Their funereal progress was almost as slow as the glaciers which formed the valleys through which many of the lines ran. In fact, to quote Ahrons: 'Why it was ever allowed to be called a railway is beyond comprehension.' Allied to the fact that its Board was extremely cantankerous and ready at any moment for an argument in defence of an indefensible position—more Aberdeen granite perhaps, as recounted earlier. It was in every sense the Scottish equivalent of the Lancashire and Yorkshire Railway and to a lesser extent, the South Eastern: all were birds of a feather.

The Parliamentary fare of the period was 1d. per mile, but the G.N. of S. managed to extract 50 per cent. more than this from Scottish sporrans in order to travel on their 'express glaciers'. With an average speed of 12 to 15 miles per hour it is difficult to imagine this painful extraction, even though it was quicker than walking! One further subtle means of relieving the weight from a wallet was the abolition of second class travel, some 20 years before the Midland Railway, and for the third, or tourist class travel, a fare was charged which was above the previous second class one. The company were compelled by law to run what was known as a 'Government' train at the Parliamentary fare, but it contrived to run this so early that most self-respecting people were still in bed. The best 'express' train prior to 1880 took 255 minutes for the 80¼ miles from Aberdeen to Elgin, an average speed of almost 19 miles per hour, and this over a road which was by no means a difficult one. The return trains were even worse, with an average only slightly above 17 miles per hour. For some unaccountable reason a third train called at a distillery and for their pains the through passengers managed to remain on board for 375 minutes, achieving an overall average speed of 12 miles per hour!

Trains on the Peterhead line were a little better, with a best average speed of 20½ miles per hour, whilst the Ballater service required more care to maintain a reasonable average, and punctuality, in view of the influential people living along the line. After Mr. Moffat took over as General Manager in 1880 there was a considerable revolution, and with the able assistance of Messrs. Reid, the passenger superintendent, and James Manson, the locomotive superintendent, the company gradually became the railway it was supposed to be. By 1888, even with the difficulties inherent with long stretches of single track, the average speed of the better trains was around 40 miles per hour, and in the later years of its existence the fastest services were approaching 50 miles per hour. The parallel with the Lancashire and Yorkshire Railway is not an idle one and stands to show what an able management could achieve in obtaining quick, reliable and comfortable services. One small, but significant, change was the introduction by Manson of an automatic tablet exchange system for single line block working, and this must be rated a contributory factor in the general speeding-up of services.

The train services on the Highland were of a completely different character with its long main line from, effectively, Perth to Wick, a length only a few miles shorter than the L.N.W.R. main line from Euston to Carlisle. In fact, the Highland Railway was, to all intents and purposes, a 'main line' railway with very few branches. Eventually the Perth-Inverness line was shortened by 26 miles when the Aviemore cut-off was opened, although this did not reduce the journey time to any great extent, involving as it did the long climb over Slochd summit, only 150 ft. less than its highest at Druimuachdar. It was also hampered with an inconvenient terminus at Inverness and through services were only achieved by attaching the odd coach to the through mail trains. Despite its steeply-graded main line it did, in the early days, far outrun the G.N. of S. by having one service averaging 25 miles per hour for the run from Perth to Inverness. It was this train which was considerably better patronised than the statutory 'Government' one, which was no better than that of the G.N. of S; this averaged just over 17 miles per hour and took over 8 hours for the journey. It must be remembered that in those far-off days there were neither corridors nor heating available to the traveller and a winter journey was not to be undertaken lightly. Foot warmers would be an essential part of one's luggage.

There were no fast services to Wick, and the best a traveller could do was to choose the early Sunday morning departure from Inverness. With the general Scottish adherence to the sanctity of the Sabbath the company contrived to maintain this reverence by cutting the normal schedule from 9½ hours to 7½. Even with due regard to this, the services to Wick were very meagre. The ones on the line to Kyle, from Keith, were just as meagre, and normally involved at least two changes, and in some cases three. The improvements in services began in earnest when the Perth-Inverness run was cut to 4 hours with an overall average speed of 36 miles per hour, which was very good running for single line working over this heavily-graded line. With the advent of improved motive power the service showed only a marginal improvement, even after the cut-off was opened and several sections doubled. The service to Wick was also improved but remained considerably slower.

The Highland had two major enemies—apart from its troubles with the G.N. of S. These were firstly, its connections with the Caledonian and North British services at Perth;

and secondly snow. The first revolved around the punctuality of the incoming trains, and in this respect the North British were by no stretch of the imagination perfect. Any unpunctuality could result in utter chaos on the single line, and in many cases hasty telegraphy had to be resorted to to ensure safe working. The variable arrivals of the fishing fleets at the northern extremities of the line approximated the unpunctuality at the southern end with the same result. One more factor comes into the reckoning at this stage. The Scottish highlands have always been a major centre for the annual shoot and for a period at the end of July and early August, Inverness and points North were, for about seven weeks, cluttered up with a multifarious collection of 'foreign' rolling stock which it could hardly cater for. At the end of the seven weeks the foreigners migrated southwards, congesting the main line and rather like a flock of pigeons, descended on Perth for dispersal.

After the shooting season migration the railway went into its normal state of semi-hibernation for the winter, and here the second enemy hove into sight. This was the snow and the blizzards where, on the more exposed areas, goods trains sometimes went into total hibernation for several weeks by being buried in the drifts. To counter this, snow fences were built to stop excessive drifting and later special blowers were constructed in the worst-affected areas where even the snow fences were inadequate.

The first locomotive superintendent of the G.N. of S. was D.K. Clark, who was more of a consulting engineer than he was resident. The first engines of the company were designed by him and built by Messrs. Fairbairn. They incorporated an unusual feature which was to remain with the company for a long time; this was a smoke prevention system whereby air was let into the sides of the firebox and jets of steam were used to induce distribution of the air above the fire. Whilst this worked well, it is apparent that his locomotives on the whole did not, and, following an argument over his supervision of the building, he resigned in July 1855. His place was taken by John Ruthven who resigned the post in 1857 after yet another squabble amongst the Directors. He was succeeded by W. Cowan, whose main products were to follow the general designs of D.K. Clark. However, he did have a comparatively quiet time until yet another squabble ensued in 1883 and he too resigned. James Manson took over the office and remained until 1891 when he resigned to join the Glasgow and South Western Railway. Clark's smoke prevention device was still in use during Manson's term of office, although modified, but he was the originator of more capable locomotives than those of his predecessors. His successor was James Johnson, whose father S.W. Johnson held the corresponding post at Derby, and from that date several Midland Railway features started to appear on his designs. His main contribution was to design what was basically a standard 4-4-0 tender locomotive for the system, both for passenger and goods, a trend which was followed when his position was taken by William Pickersgill in 1894. The latter's main contribution was to introduce the side window cab for greater protection for the enginemen. The last holder of the post was Thomas Haywood who took over the reins in 1914, but whose talents were not to be shown, except for four small dock engines, due to the economies of the First World War and its after-effects.

All the tender locomotives of the company were four-coupled and were, in the main for mixed traffic use. Only once were six-coupled engines in evidence, and these were only nine in number; these were built by Kitson & Co. to Manson's design and used on the Aberdeen suburban services to Dyce and Culter. The majority were built to the 4-4-0 wheel arrangement with the odd excursion to 0-4-4 tanks. The G.N. of S. were one of the pioneers of railmotors, two being designed by Pickersgill in 1905 to work the Lossiemouth and St. Combs branches. Even though the company were concerned at the cost of operating these branches by conventional motive power, the units were not successful and by 1906 had been taken out of regular use. Only once was 6 ft. 1 in. exceeded for the size of the driving wheels; these were on the three engines of class Q which had 6 ft. 6½ in. wheels. At least followers of the G.N. of S. have the satisfaction of knowing that old number 49 'Gordon Highlander', one of the last batch of locomotives built for the line, is now preserved. These engines were basically the same design as the class S onwards, a Johnson design. Although attributed to Heywood they were really a continuation of his rebuilding of the 45 engines of classes S, T and V. The original locomotive works were at Kittybrewster, which was far too small for its purpose—only holding four engines for repair—and in consequence all the locomotives were outside built until Manson managed, by means unknown, to build two locomotives in 1887. Eventually a new works was opened at Inverurie in 1903, but it was only in 1909 that the first company-built locomotives appeared.

On the Highland Railway, the first locomotive superintendent to appear was William Barclay, of the earlier Inverness and Nairn Railway. He was the nephew of Alexander Allen of Crewe fame and consequently the Allen 'Crewe Type' became the optimum design and one which lasted almost to the end of David Jones's period of office in 1896, albeit in more modern form. The bulk of Barclay's designs were of the Allen 2-2-2 wheel arrangement but most were rebuilt as 2-4-0s after 1864 when the Forres-Perth line was opened. He resigned in 1865 and his place was taken by William Stroudley, later to achieve fame on the London, Brighton and South Coast Railway. His only real claim to fame on the Highland was that the genesis of his famous 'Terriers' was designed during his term of office. He, in turn, resigned in 1869 and was replaced by David Jones. He it was who turned out the first 4-4-0 on the line in 1874; but it is notable that the Crewe type still persisted, with outside cylinders and smokebox front always at right angles to the centre line of the cylinders. Another notable feature introduced during his reign was the peculiar cast-in louvre on the chimney front. This chimney was, in fact, a double one and the louvred outer casing was intended to induce a strong up-current of air to counteract the effect of the strong winds prevalent in the area so that a more even draught was maintained in the firebox. This remained a feature of his designs throughout his period in office, and which was also present on his last, and most famous, design. This was in 1894, when he introduced the first 4-6-0 in the country; a type probably as typically British as the 4-4-0. Here too we are fortunate in that one of the type, No. 103, has been preserved.

Jones retired in 1896 and was succeeded by Peter Drummond, the younger brother of Dugald who was in charge at the Eastleigh works of the London and South Western Railway. There was now a wind of change as typical Drummond features began to appear. Outside cylinders disappeared in favour of inside, and the normal Highland squared cabs, introduced by Stroudley, also disappeared. However, he did revert to outside cylinders for his 'Castle' class of 1900. He resigned in 1912 to take over the post which his brother had earlier held at St. Rollox, and was succeeded by Frederick Smith. His period in office was short, and in 1915 he resigned following the decision to sell his powerful, and well-engineered 'River' class 4-6-0s to the Caledonian Railway. This was brought about by the decision of the Company's civil engineer that they were too heavy for the track. His place was taken by Christopher Cumming whose most notable contributions were the 'Clan' 4-6-0s and the smaller-wheeled goods version, both excellent performers, neatly proportioned and which lasted into British Railway days. He resigned for health reasons in 1922. It is perhaps ironic that the Smith engines returned to the Highland in the post-grouping period and proved excellent performers. The locomotive works were at Lochgorm, situated in the triangle north of Inverness station. Despite the fact that the works were by no means as cramped as those at Kittybrewster, the Highland were heavily committed to outside builders. One peculiarity of the Highland was that when locomotives disappeared into Lochgorm works they had a bad habit of re-appearing with new names, for no apparent reason, and since all Highland passenger engines carried names which were of the transfer pattern it would seem possible that an old version of 'scrabble' may have been used to cover the transfers in stock. It was, however, noticeable that when moves were made to a different locality then names associated with the area were put on. Fortunately this practice ceased towards the end of the 19th century.

Of the management of the two companies, little need be said to augment what has gone before. Mr. Moffat of the G.N. of S. has already been mentioned. On the Highland an important figure was to emerge on that company's board; this was William, later Sir William, Whitelaw who twice held the chairmanship of the company, and who later held the same office on the London and North Eastern Railway. Also on the Highland was its first, and famous, chairman Alexander Matheson and Mr. Park, its General Manager during the hectic wartime period.

Before leaving the managerial question it will be of interest to look into this aspect at the time of the annual shoot. As recounted in the working section of these notes, the myriad collection of vehicles which used to congregate at the various sidings must have created many headaches for both the operating staff and also for the traffic superintendent. This pilgrimage should have been subject to Board of Trade regulations as far as the length and the make-up of its trains were concerned. From the goings-on it would seem that since the bureaucrats were a long way away in the precincts of Whitehall, that the regulations were read with both eyes closed. The result was that the trains were made up in whatever order suited the staff, whose prime concern was to get rid of them as soon as possible. Nor in these instances were they in any sense specials! It is recounted by Foxwell in 1888 that one train left Perth made up of 36 vehicles, although it must be remembered that the entire train would be of six-wheeled stock, with the exception of some four-wheeled horse boxes. It consisted of nine companies' vehicles marshalled in a haphazard order—at least at the front of the train—but it is most noticeable that all the Highland stock was at the rear so that all the major strain on the couplings was taken by other companies' stock. In all probability the company was breaking a Board of Trade regulation with respect to the length of the train, but a further regulation was that the B.O.T. objected to banking engines, preferring pilot engines instead. However, they had both; the Highland complied by providing a pilot engine and also (probably to protect its own vehicles at the rear of the train from running back on the gradients in the event of a coupling breaking) a banking engine also. This train must have made an impressive sight clambering over Druimuachdar. It is not recounted whether any of the bureaucrats were entrained, but if they were they were probably more concerned with getting to the firing range.

Despite the mountainous nature of the area, and the many river valleys to be traversed, neither company could boast of any major structures to rival those of the companies further south. This is not to say that there were no major engineering works; there were many of these with several deep and long cuttings cut out of solid rock. The G.N. of S. managed to travel along most of the river valleys with little major bridging work required. On the Highland, the line tended to follow the contour with the consequence that it had many fairly steep gradients and quite sharp curvature. The provision of only a single line of railway helped to reduce the severity of the excavations and earthworks, and on the entire line there were only three tunnels. Despite this there were several viaducts over the river estuaries which were quite long and high. One, however, which deserves mention was well inland, near Slochd summit, where a masonry viaduct of eight arches with a maximum height of over 100 ft. was erected. What is considered to make this one particularly worthy of note is that at each end of the viaduct deep rock cuttings had to be made before even a viaduct of comparatively modest dimensions could be built.

It will be appreciated that it is impossible to cover every aspect of a company's history in this short account and reference should be made to the more complete works mentioned in the Introduction. Whilst these two companies were amongst the smaller ones, this does not make them in any way less interesting.

In the interest of completeness it is necessary to mention the Brora colliery tramway of 1 ft. 8 in. gauge, which, whilst having no physical connection with the Highland Railway, had exchange sidings to the north of Brora station. The first phase in the history of this line was the opening of a colliery on the South side of the river Brora to the harbour. This was closed about 1810 and a new colliery opened on the north side of the river under the patronage of the Duke of Sutherland. This line joined the earlier harbour line by means of a bridge over the river close to the present railway bridge. When the Highland Railway was opened to beyond Brora, a works (now a woollen mill) and exchange sidings were built. Traffic failed to come up to expectations and the line was finally closed in 1947 and subsequently dismantled. The colliery workings were on the west side of the later railway.

* * * * * * * * * * * * * * * *

(a) Great North of Scotland Railway

	By Act	Date
GREAT NORTH OF SCOTLAND RLY	Inc 9 & 10 Vic cap 103	26-6-46
the GN of S purchased the		
ABERDEENSHIRE CANAL	Inc 36 Geo III cap 68	26-4-1796
in 1845 for part of its route		
without parliamentary authority		

AMALGAMATIONS

		By Act	Date
1.	KEITH & DUFFTOWN RLY	Inc 20 & 21 Vic cap 87	27-7-57
	re-authorized to amended route	23 Vic cap 63	25-5-60
	amalg with GN of S	29 & 30 Vic cap 288	30-7-66
2.	STRATHSPEY RLY	Inc 24 Vic cap 16	17-5-61
	amalg with GN of S	29 & 30 Vic cap 288	30-7-66
3.	BANFF, MACDUFF & TURRIFF JCN RLY	Inc 18 Vic cap 57	15-6-55
	change of name (19.4.59.) to		
	ABERDEEN & TURRIFF RLY	22 Vic cap 11	19-4-59
	amalg with GN of S	29 & 30 Vic cap 288	30-7-66
4.	BANFF, MACDUFF & TURRIFF EXTENSION RLY	Inc 20 & 21 Vic cap 50	27-7-57
	amalg with GN of S	29 & 30 Vic cap 288	30-7-66
5.	ALFORD VALLEY RLY	Inc 9 & 10 Vic cap 134	3-7-46
	powers lapsed after railway		
	mania and company—	Re-inc 19 Vic cap 40	26-3-56
	amalg with GN of S	29 & 30 Vic cap 288	30-7-66
6.	INVERURY (sic) & OLD MELDRUM JCN RLY	Inc 18 Vic cap 65	15-6-55
	leased to GN of S from 1.9.57	21 Vic cap 45	14-6-58
	amalg with GN of S	29 & 30 Vic cap 288	30-7-66
7.	FORMARTINE & BUCHAN RLY	Inc 21 & 22 Vic cap 108	23-7-58
	acquired by GN of S	29 & 30 Vic cap 288	30-7-66
	Amalgamation powers under Act 29 & 30 Vic cap 288 effective from 31.7.66.		
8.	BANFF, PORTSOY & STRATHISLA RLY	Inc 20 & 21 Vic cap 53	27-7-57
	worked by GN of S from 1.2.63		
	change of name (21.7.63.) to		
	BANFFSHIRE RLY	26 & 27 Vic cap 170	21-7-63
	amalg with GN of S	30 & 31 Vic cap 190	12-8-67
	retrospective to 31.7.67.		
9.	DEESIDE RLY	Inc 9 & 10 Vic cap 158	16-7-46
	company dissolved and—	Re-inc 15 Vic cap 61	28-5-52
	amalg with GN of S	39 & 40 Vic cap 124	13-7-76
	retrospective to 31.8.75.		
	DEESIDE EXTENSION RLY	20 & 21 Vic cap 49	27-7-57
	(under Deeside Rly Further Powers Act)		
	amalg with GN of S	39 & 40 Vic cap 124	13-7-76
	retrospective to 31.8.75.		

	By Act	Date
10. ABOYNE & BRAEMAR RLY	Inc 28 & 29 Vic cap 279	5-7-65
amalg with GN of S	39 & 40 Vic cap 124	13-7-76
retrospective to 31.1.76.		
11. MORAYSHIRE RLY	Inc 9 & 10 Vic cap 178	16-7-46
transferred to GN of S	44 & 45 Vic cap 201	11-8-81
retrospective to 1.10.80.		
12. DYCE & FRASERBURGH RLY	9 & 10 Vic cap 135	3-7-46
Inc as 'Great North of Scotland		
(Eastern Extension) Rly'		
(included branch to Peterhead)		
powers lapsed and company wound-up.		
As built:		
DYCE TO PETERHEAD	21 & 22 Vic cap 108	23-7-58
(Formartine & Buchan Rly Act)		
Maud Jcn to Fraserburgh		
—deviation of original route, authorized		
by Formartine & Buchan Rly Act	26 & 27 Vic cap 189	21-7-63

LINES PROMOTED BY GN OF S

CRUDEN RLY	56 & 57 Vic cap 201	24-8-93
as 'Cruden Section' authorized by	(GN of S Act)	
GN of S Further Powers Act		

LIGHT RLY

FRASERBURGH & ST COMBS	Light Railway Order	8-9-99
Constructed and worked by the GN of S		

JOINT COMMITTEE

GN of S/Scottish North Eastern Rly (C.R.)		
DENBURN VALLEY RAILWAY	27 & 28 Vic cap 111	23-6-64
connection at Aberdeen & joint station		
(Scottish North Eastern Rly Act)		
GN of S Powers to Subscribe)		

(b) Highland Railway

HIGHLAND RAILWAY		
Formed	28 & 29 Vic cap 168	29-6-65
with effect from 1.8.65. (Sect 1 of Act)		
by amalgamation of:		
1. INVERNESS & ABERDEEN JCN RLY	Inc 19 & 20 Vic cap 110	21-7-56
2. INVERNESS & PERTH JCN RLY	Inc 24 & 25 Vic cap 186	22-7-61
Both companies being legally dissolved		
from commencement of Act (Sect 6).		

	By Act	Date

AMALGAMATIONS EFFECTED BY
CONSTITUENT COMPANIES

		By Act	Date
1. (a)	INVERNESS & NAIRN RLY	Inc 17 & 18 Vic cap 176	24-7-54
	amalg with Inverness & Aberdeen Jcn	24 Vic cap 8	17-5-61
(b)	INVERNESS & ROSS—SHIRE RLY	Inc 23 & 24 Vic cap 131	3-7-60
	amalg with Inverness & Aberdeen Jcn	25 & 26 Vic cap 113	30-6-62
2. (a)	PERTH & DUNKELD RLY	Inc 17 & 18 Vic cap 148	10-7-54
	amalg with Inverness & Perth Jcn from 28.2.64.	26 Vic cap 58	8-6-63

AMALGAMATIONS

		By Act	Date
1.	DINGWALL & SKYE RLY	Inc 28 & 29 Vic cap 223	5-7-65
	amalg with Highland Rly effective from 1.9.80.	43 & 44 Vic cap 129	2-8-80
2.	SUTHERLAND RLY	Inc 28 & 29 Vic cap 169	29-6-65
	amalg with Highland Rly effective from 1.9.84.	47 & 48 Vic cap 184	28-7-84
3.	SUTHERLAND & CAITHNESS RLY	Inc 34 & 35 Vic cap 99	13-7-71
	amalg with Highland Rly effective from 1.9.84.	47 & 48 Vic cap 184	28-7-84

INDEPENDENT UNDERTAKINGS

		By Act	Date
1.	Construction of privately-owned railways Golspie-Helmsdale by the Duke of Sutherland—authorized.	33 & 34 Vic cap 31	20-6-70
	Taken over by Highland Railway	47 & 48 Vic cap 184	28-7-84
2.	FINDHORN RLY	Inc 22 Vic cap 8	19-4-59
	worked as branch by Inverness & Aberdeen Jcn from 1.3.62. Not amalgamated with either I. & A.J. or Highland Rly. Board of Trade Defunct Companies List shows as being out of use by 1869 but there is evidence to indicate sporadic usage up to 1880. Company wound-up but not under parliamentary powers.		

LIGHT RAILWAYS

			Date
1.	WICK & LYBSTER LIGHT RLY	Light Railway Order	27-11-99
2.	DORNOCH LIGHT RLY	Light Railway Order	13-8-98

Both lines constructed and worked as an integral part of the Highland Railway.

* * * * * * * * * * * * * * * * *

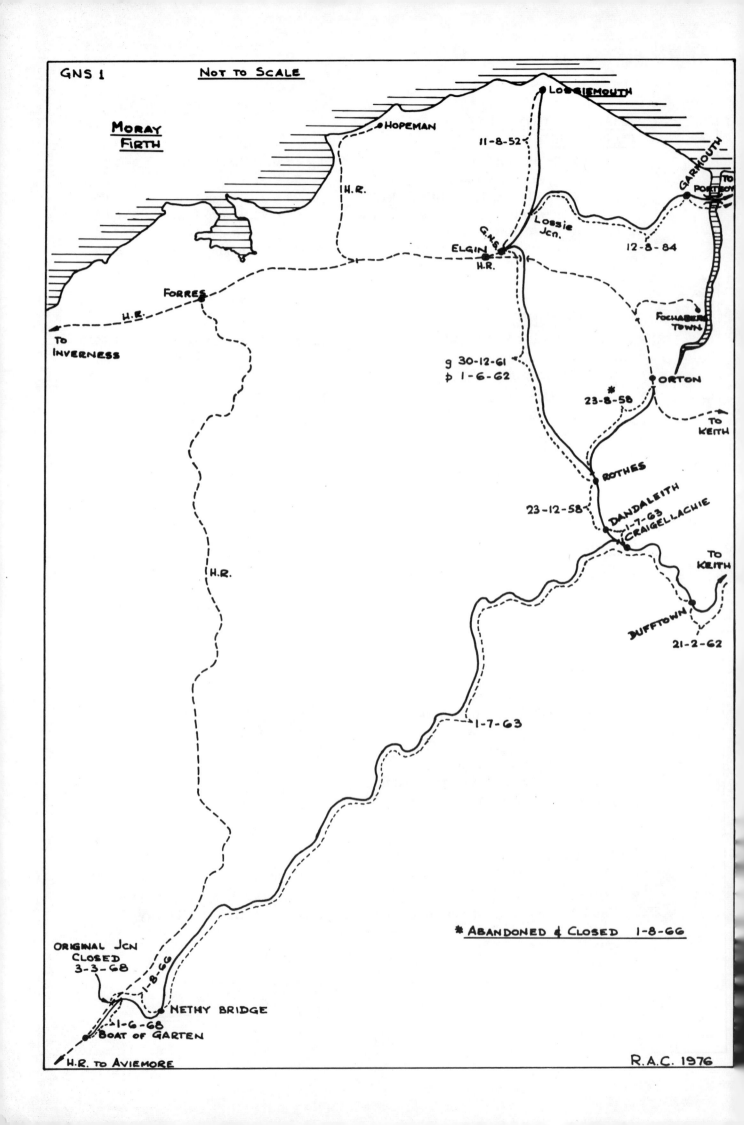

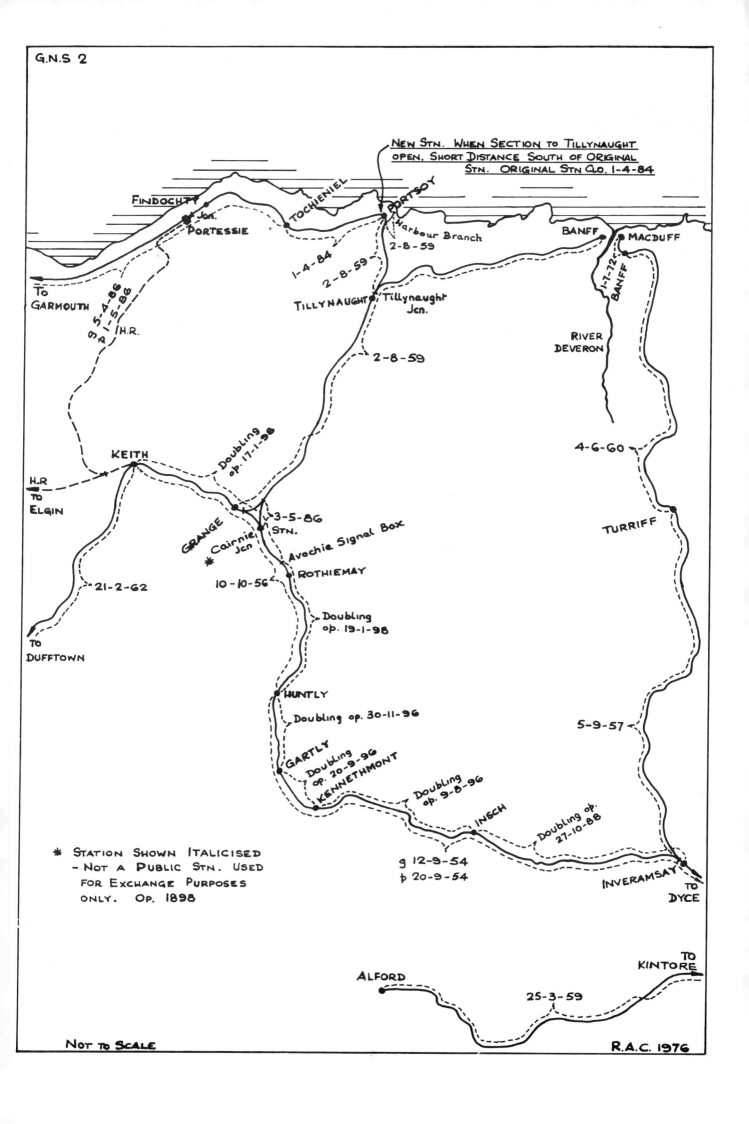

G.N.S 2

NEW STN. WHEN SECTION TO TILLYNAUGHT
OPEN, SHORT DISTANCE SOUTH OF ORIGINAL
STN. ORIGINAL STN CLO. 1-4-84

FINDOCHTY
TOCHIENIEL
PORTSOY
PORTESSIE Jcn.
Harbour Branch
2-8-59
BANFF
MACDUFF

1-4-84
2-8-59

TO
GARMOUTH
3·5·4·86
H.R.
9·1-5·86

TILLYNAUGHT
Tillynaught
Jcn.
2-8-59

1-7-72
BANFF

RIVER
DEVERON

Doubling
op. 17-1-98

KEITH

4-6-60

H.R
TO
ELGIN

GRANGE
3-5-86
STN.
Cairnie
Jcn.
Avochie Signal Box

TURRIFF

21-2-62
10-10-56
ROTHIEMAY

TO
DUFFTOWN

Doubling
op. 19-1-98

HUNTLY

Doubling op. 30-11-96

5-9-57

GARTLY
Doubling
op. 20-9-96
KENNETHMONT
Doubling
op. 9-8-96
INSCH
Doubling op.
27-10-88

* STATION SHOWN ITALICISED
– NOT A PUBLIC STN. USED
FOR EXCHANGE PURPOSES
ONLY. OP. 1898

g 12-9-54
þ 20-9-54

INVERAMSAY
TO
DYCE

TO
KINTORE

ALFORD
25-3-59

NOT TO SCALE
R.A.C. 1976

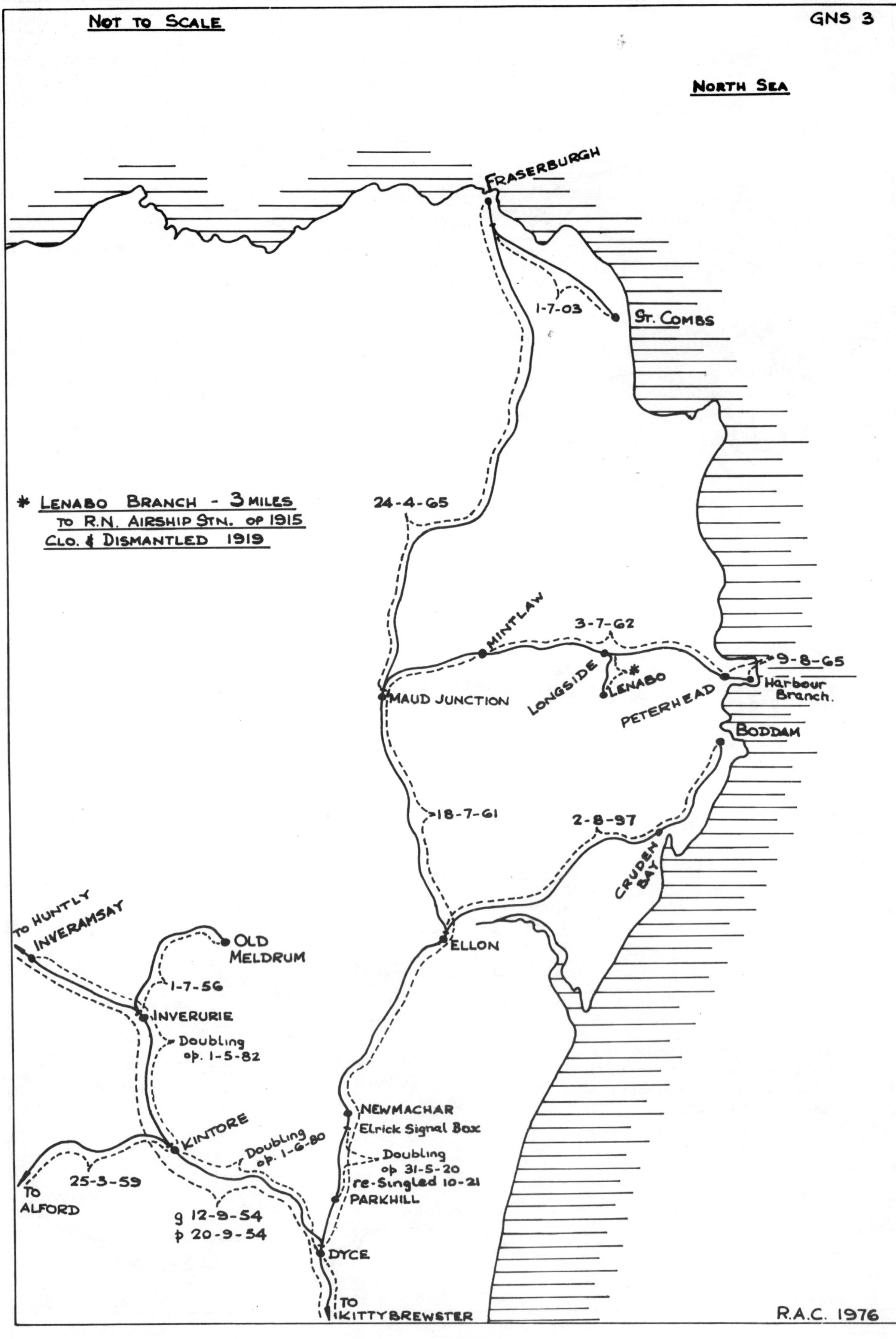

NOT TO SCALE

NORTH SEA

FRASERBURGH

1-7-03

St. COMBS

24-4-65

* LENABO BRANCH - 3 MILES
  TO R.N. AIRSHIP STN. op 1915
  CLO. & DISMANTLED 1919

MINTLAW

3-7-62

9-8-65

LONGSIDE

* LENABO

PETERHEAD

Harbour Branch.

MAUD JUNCTION

BODDAM

18-7-61

2-8-97

CRUDEN BAY

TO HUNTLY
INVERAMSAY

OLD MELDRUM

ELLON

1-7-56

INVERURIE

Doubling
op. 1-5-82

KINTORE

NEWMACHAR
Elrick Signal Box

Doubling
op. 1-6-80

Doubling
op 31-5-20
re-Singled 10-21

25-3-59

PARKHILL

TO ALFORD

g 12-9-54
p 20-9-54

DYCE

TO KITTYBREWSTER

R.A.C. 1976

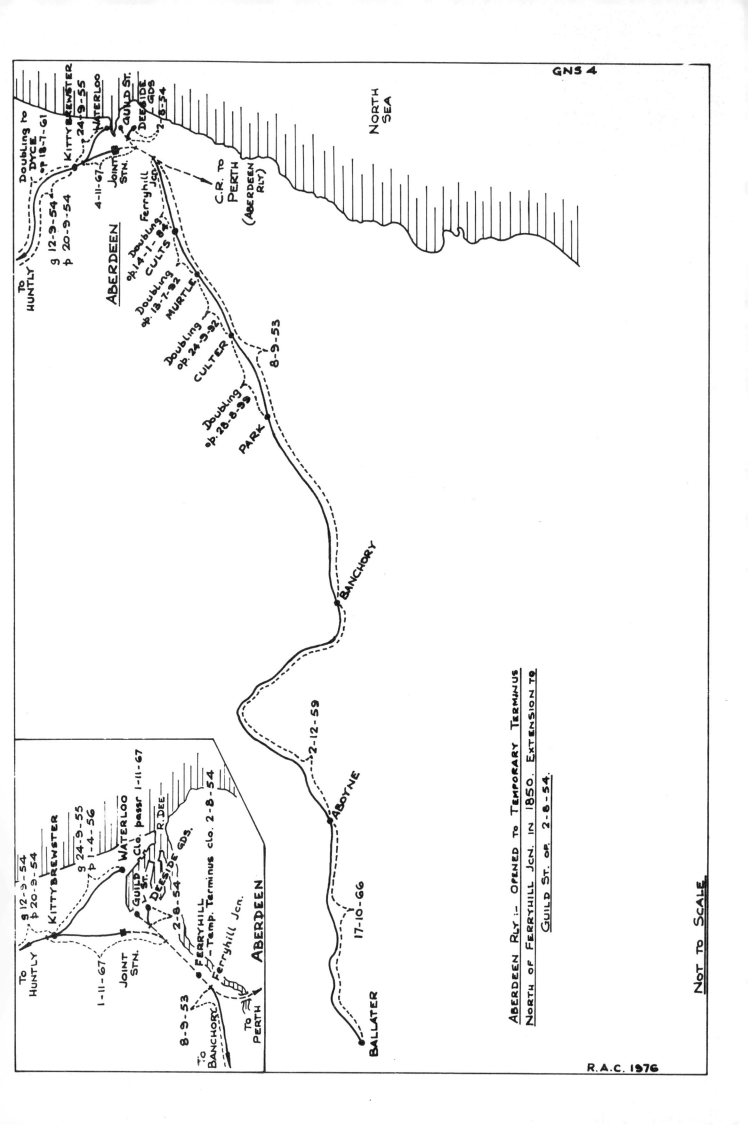

GNS 4

NORTH
SEA

To
HUNTLY

Doubling to
DYCE
op 18-7-61

KITTYBREWSTER
g 24-9-55

WATERLOO

GUILD ST.
DEESIDE
GDS
2-8-54

4-11-67

g 12-9-54
p 20-9-54

ABERDEEN

JOINT
STN.

Ferryhill Jcn.

C.R. to
PERTH
(ABERDEEN
RLY)

Doubling
op 14-1-84

CULTS

Doubling
op 13-7-92

MURTLE

Doubling
op 24-3-92

CULTER

8-9-53

Doubling
op 28-8-99

PARK

BANCHORY

2-12-59

ABOYNE

17-10-66

BALLATER

To
HUNTLY

g 12-9-54
p 20-9-54

KITTYBREWSTER

1-11-67

g 24-9-55
p 1-4-56

WATERLOO

Clo. passr 1-11-67

GUILD
ST.

DEESIDE GDS.

R. DEE

2-8-54

FERRYHILL
— Temp. Terminus clo. 2-8-54

Ferryhill Jcn.

JOINT
STN.

To
PERTH

To
BANCHORY

8-9-53

ABERDEEN

ABERDEEN RLY :- OPENED TO TEMPORARY TERMINUS
North of FERRYHILL JCN. IN 1850. EXTENSION TO
GUILD ST. OP. 2-8-54.

NOT TO SCALE

R.A.C. 1976

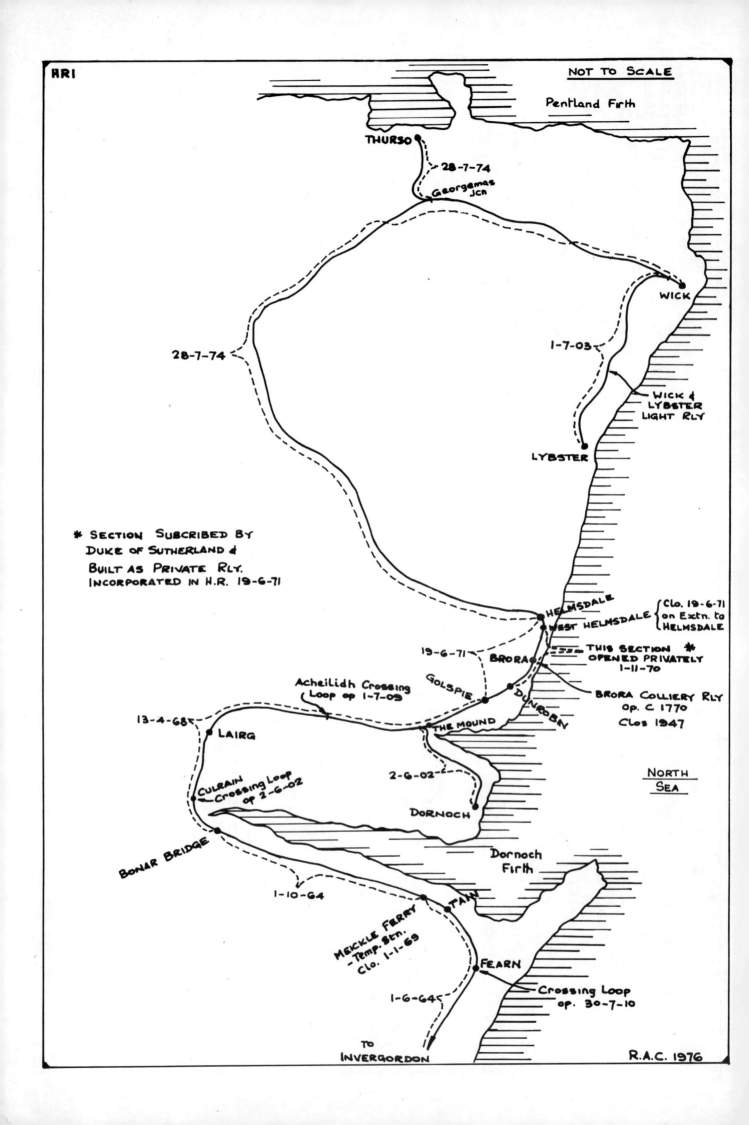

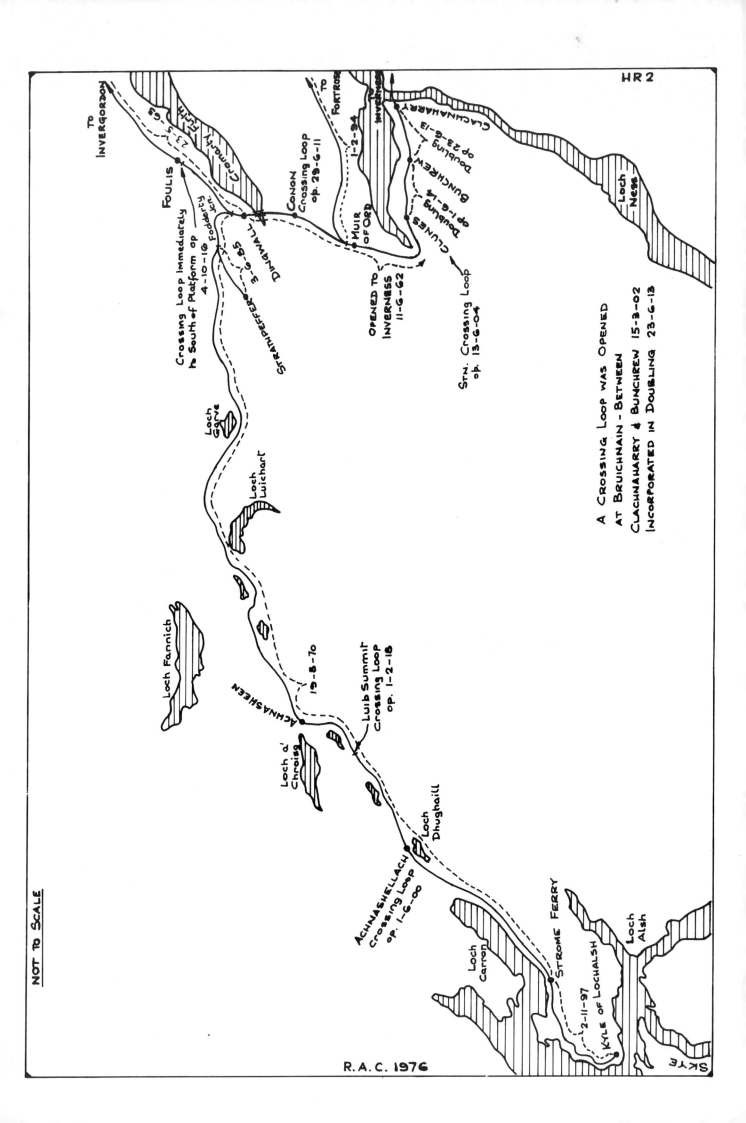

NOT TO SCALE

HR 2

To INVERGORDON

FOULIS

Crossing Loop immediately to South of Platform op 4-10-10

Cromarty Firth 23-5-63

DINGWALL

Conon Crossing Loop op. 29-6-11

Fodderty Junction

STRATHPEFFER 3-6-85

MUIR OF ORD

1-2-94

To FORTROSE

To INVERNESS

CLACHNAHARRY

Doubling op. 23-6-13

BUNCHREW

Doubling op. 1-6-14

CLUNES

Doubling op. 1-6-14

Loch Ness

OPENED TO INVERNESS 11-6-62

Stn. Crossing Loop op. 13-6-04

Loch Garve

Loch Luichart

ACHNASHEEN

Loch Fannich

15-8-70

Luib Summit Crossing Loop op. 1-2-18

A CROSSING LOOP WAS OPENED AT BRUICHNAIN - BETWEEN CLACHNAHARRY & BUNCHREW 15-3-02 INCORPORATED IN DOUBLING 23-6-13

Loch a' Chroisg

Loch Dhughaill

ACHNASHELLACH Crossing Loop op. 1-6-00

Loch Carron

STROME FERRY

2-11-97

KYLE OF LOCHALSH

Loch Alsh

SKYE

R.A.C. 1976

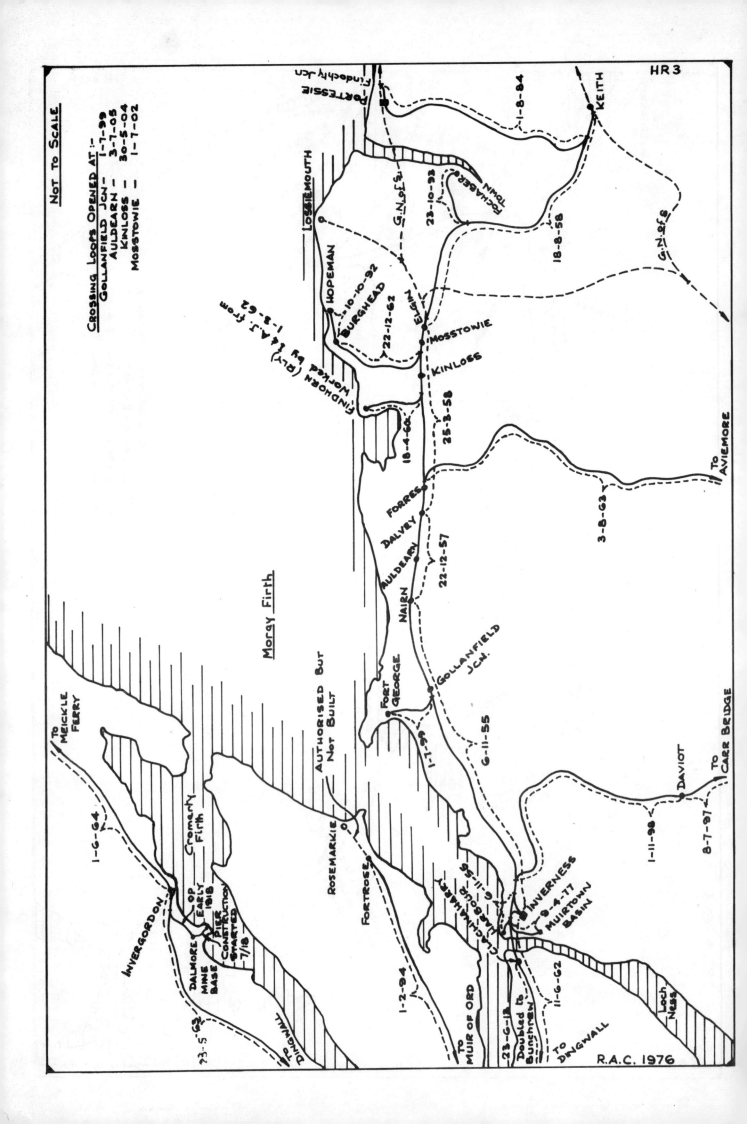

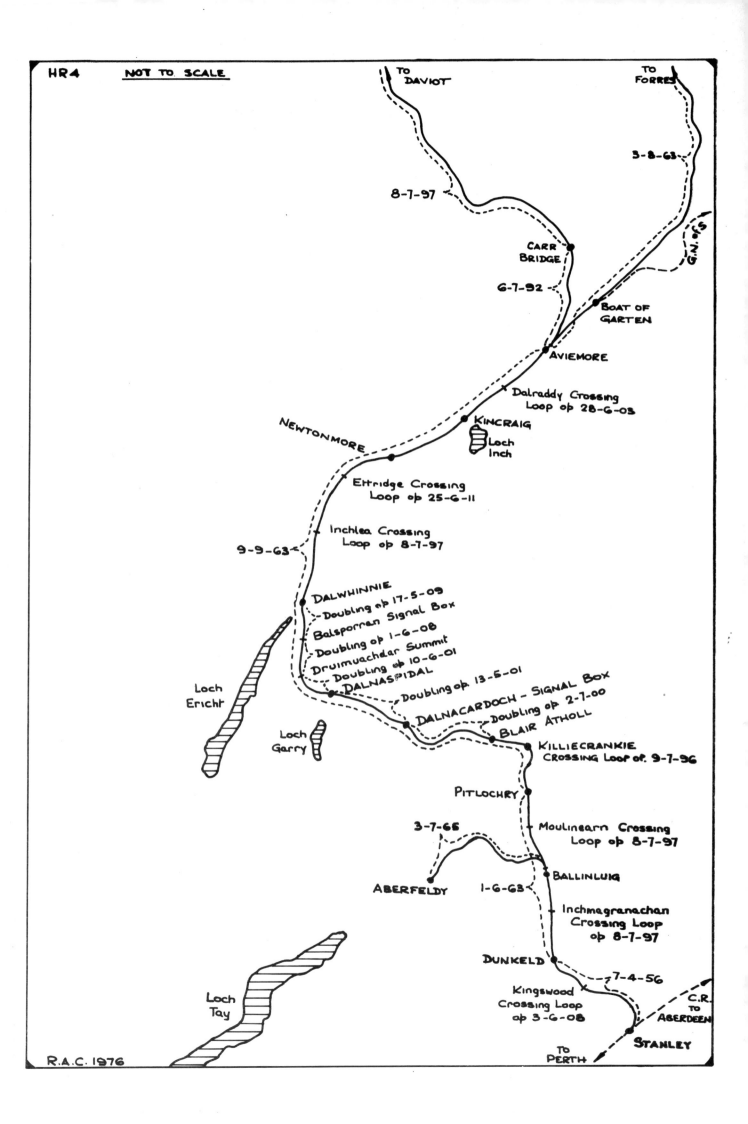

HR4   NOT TO SCALE

TO DAVIOT

TO FORRES

3-8-63

8-7-97

CARR BRIDGE

6-7-92

G.N. of S.

BOAT OF GARTEN

AVIEMORE

Dalraddy Crossing Loop op 28-6-03

NEWTONMORE

KINCRAIG

Loch Inch

Ettridge Crossing Loop op 25-6-11

Inchlea Crossing Loop op 8-7-97

9-9-63

DALWHINNIE
Doubling op 17-5-09
Balsporran Signal Box
Doubling op 1-6-08
Druimuachdar Summit
Doubling op 10-6-01
DALNASPIDAL
Doubling op 13-5-01

Loch Ericht

DALNACARDOCH – SIGNAL BOX
Doubling op 2-7-00
BLAIR ATHOLL

Loch Garry

KILLIECRANKIE
CROSSING LOOP op. 9-7-96

PITLOCHRY

3-7-65

Moulinearn Crossing Loop op 8-7-97

BALLINLUIG

ABERFELDY

1-6-63

Inchmagranachan Crossing Loop op 8-7-97

DUNKELD

7-4-56

Kingswood Crossing Loop op 3-6-08

C.R. TO ABERDEEN

Loch Tay

STANLEY

R.A.C. 1976

TO PERTH